TOASTS

COMPILED BY
WM. R. RHOADS

DRAWINGS BY—
CLARE VICTOR DWIGGINS

PHILADELPHIA
THE PENN PUBLISHING COMPANY

TOASTS

HERE'S to the stars and stripes,
To the land of our birth,
The American Girl—
The best thing on earth.

If all your beauties one by one,
  I pledge, dear, I am thinking
Before the tale were well begun
  I had been dead of drinking.

———

Could you be true to eyes of blue?
  I could, but then of late
The stacks of blue have not been true,
  So eyes of blue must wait.

———

Here's health to every nation—but Carrie.

———

Here's to my mother-in-law, God bless her—
but I don't insist upon it.

———

Here's to the Tar that sticks like pitch to
his duty.

HERE'S to matrimony —the high sea for which no compass has yet been invented.

Laugh and the world laughs with you, Weep, and the laugh's on you.

———

To woman—the bitter half of man.

———

To marriage—which is like a beleaguered fortress; those who are without want to get in, and those within want to get out.

———

Woman—She needs no eulogy; she speaks for herself.

The Sphere
of Woman

THEY talk about a woman's sphere
as though it had a limit;
There's not a place on earth or heaven,
There's not a task to mankind given,
There's not a blessing or a woe,
There's not a whispered yes or no,
There's not a life or birth,
That has a feather's weight of worth
Without a woman in it.

Here's to the hand of
friendship,
Sincere, twice-tried and true,
That smiles in the hour of triumph
And laughs at its joy with you,
Yet stands in the night of sorrow
Close by when the shadows fall,
And never turns the picture
Of an old friend to the wall.

———

Here's to that most fascinating woman, the
widow of some other man!

———

Were't the last drop in the well
As I gasped upon the brink,
Ere my fainting spirit fell
'Tis to thee that I would drink!

———

Here's luck, and hopin' God will take a
likin' to us!

MAY bad fortune follow you
all your days
And never catch up with you.

 to the Wit who cracks his jokes in a
nutshell.

To the " Auto "—May we hear its toot
In time to scoot.

May we all come to peaceful ends,
And leave our debts unto our friends.

Here's to the Doctor who " brought us,"
Here's to the Mother who taught us,
Here's to our Rivals who fought us,
And here's to the Maiden who caught us.

To Woman—When man was made, God sent a
helper to him;
And so she proved, for she helped to
undo him.

J you live as long as you like,
And have what you like as long as you live.

unshine and good humor all the world over.

———

To our absent friends.

———

" To all who put their trust in God—but never their God in a trust."

———

Through this toilsome world, alas !
Once, and only once we pass:
If a kindness we may show,
If a good deed we may do
To our suffering fellow-men,
Let us do it when we can,
Nor delay it, for 'tis plain,
We shall not pass this way again.

HERE'S rest for the weary,
In peace rest his
soul;
Good luck to
the wanderer
Who's lost the keyhole!

Woman: A Mistress of Arts, who robs a bachelor of his degree, and forces him to study philosophy by means of curtain lectures.

———

For though they almost blush to reign,
Though love's own flowers wreathe the chain,
Disguise the bondage as we will,
'Tis woman—woman rules us still.

———

May the blossoms of love never be blighted,
And a true-hearted young woman never be slighted.

———

May our injuries be written in sand and our friendships in marble.

Here's to a long life and
a merry one;
A quick death, and a
painless one;
A pretty girl, and a
loving one;
A cold bottle, and
another one.

———

May we never murmur without cause,
And never have cause to murmur.

———

Happy are we met, happy have we been,
Happy may we part, and happy meet again.

———

While we live, let's live in clover,
For when we're dead, we're dead all over.

The Boundaries of Our Country—East, by the Rising Sun; north, by the North Pole; west, by all Creation; and south, by the Day of Judgment.

America—My native land. I turn to you,
>   With blessing and with prayer;
>   Where man is brave and woman true,
>   And free as mountain air.
>   Long may our flag in triumph wave
>   Against the world combined,
>   And friends a welcome—foes a grave
>   Within our borders find.

Our Country—To her we drink, for her we pray,
>   Our voices silent never;
>   For her we'll fight, come what
>   come may,
>   The Stars and Stripes forever.

HERE'S to all the world,—

For fear some darn fool may take offence.

MAY the most you wish for be the least you get.

———

The Army to the Ladies.

Our arms your defence,

Your arms our recompense.

Fall in!

HERE's to the land of the
Shamrock so green,
Here's to each lad and
his darling colleen,
Here's to the ones
we love dearest and most—
And may God save old Ireland!
That's an Irishman's toast.

———

Here's to those who love us,
And here's to those who don't,
A smile for those who are willing to,
And a tear for those who won't.

———

Love to one, Friendship to a few, and Good-
will to all.

———

Here's to that sad state—Utah, " Where
a single death may make a dozen
widows."

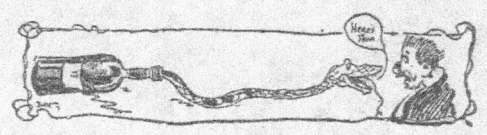

May the moon shine whene'er we dine,
And the sun instead, when we go to bed.

———

May our faults be written on the seashore, and
every good action prove a wave to wash them out.

———

May the faults of our neighbors be dim, and their
virtues glaring.

———

May the gates of consolation be ever open to the
children of affliction.

———

May we never hurt our neighbor's peace
by the desire to appear witty.

 a health to all good
lasses,
Pledge it merrily, fill your
glasses,
Let the bumper toast go round;
May they live in tranquil pleasure—
Without mixture, without measure—
For with them true joys are found.

Saint Patrick was a gentleman,
Who, through strategy and stealth,
Drove all the snakes from Ireland—
Here's a bumper to his health.
But, not too many bumpers,
Lest we lose ourselves, and then,
Forget the good Saint Patrick,
And see the snakes again.

May we bury our sorrows in a friendly draught.

———

May poverty be always a day's march behind us.

———

Everything comes to him who hustles while he waits.

———

To Our Country—We have toasted all names and places,
We've toasted all kinds of game;
Why not, just for loyalty's sake,
Drink one to our nation's name?

———

May your children have rich parents.

Here's to the memory
of George Washington,
The childless father
of eighty millions.

HERE'S to the American Aigle,
That beautiful burd so hale;
Whom nobody can invaigle
And put salt on his lovely tail.

———

To Poverty—He who in his pocket has no money,
Should, in his mouth, be never without honey.

———

The greatest gift, a woman's heart.

———

Here's to the virtue that directs our actions with
respect to ourselves ; justice to those with whom we
deal ; mercy, love, and charity to all mankind.

———

To the Home—The place where children have
their own way, and married men
resort when they have nowhere
else to keep themselves.

Here's to the light that lies
in woman's eyes——
and lies, and lies, and lies

HERE's to you that makes me
wear old clothes;
Here's to you that turns
my friends to foes—
But seeing you're so near—here goes!

———

Here's to the hostess who has worried all day,
And trembled lest everything go the wrong way;
May the grace of contentment possess her at once,
May her guests and her servants—all do the right stunts.

———

Here's lovers two to the maiden true,
And four to the maid caressing;
But the wayward girl with the lips that curl
Keeps twenty lovers guessing.

Voltaire says: "Man is the only animal that laughs, drinks when he is not thirsty, and makes love at all seasons of the year."

HERE'S a health
　　　　in homely
　　　　rhyme,
To our oldest classmate, Father Time;
May our last survivor live to be
As bald and as wise and as tough as he!

Here's to the girl behind the man
behind the gun.

———

Here's to the rich man because he is rich,
  And here's to the man that's poor.
But rich man or poor man it matters not which,
  When we're dead we're all dead ones
      That's sure.

———

Drink to fair woman, who, I think,
  Is most entitled to it;
For if anything ever can drive me to drink
  She certainly could do it.

———

Our National Paradox—The American
  Eagle:
A bird of freedom that permits no
  liberties.

Here's to the Bachelor, so lonely and gay;
    For it's not his fault, he was born that way.
    And here's to the Spinster, so lonely and
        good;
    For it's not her fault, she hath done what
        she could.

———

May we never break a joke to crack a reputation.

———

Man is somewhat like a sausage,
    Very smooth upon the skin;
But you can never tell exactly
    How much hog there is within.

———

May we always enjoy the end of a feast better
than the beginning of a fray.

———

May every honest man make money, and
be wise enough to keep it.

Clare Victor
Dwiggins

God made the world—and rested,
God made man—and rested,
Then God made woman.
Since then neither God nor man has rested.

HERE'S to the Present Moment.
Do not borrow
Tomorrow's sorrow,
Nor delay
With play today.

————

May we never lose a friend for a jest.

————

To the sun that warmed the vineyard,
To the juice that turned to wine,
To the host who cracked the bottle,
And made it yours and mine.

————

May the morality of individuals become
the policy of nations.

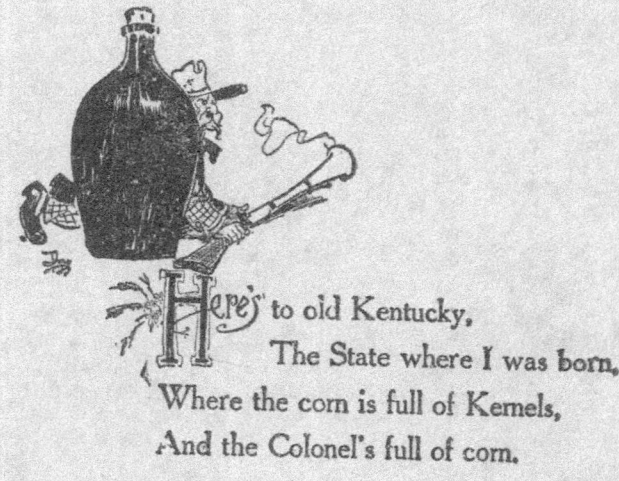

Here's to old Kentucky,
    The State where I was born,
Where the corn is full of Kernels,
And the Colonel's full of corn.

———

May the Lord love us but not call us too soon.

———

Here's to our friends in adversity, and may we
never be in the same fix.

———

Here's a health to all who need it.

Here to love and unity,
Dark corners
and opportunity!

HERE'S to a good girl—
Not too good, for the
good die young,
And we don't like dead ones!

To woman's love—to man's
not akin,
For her heart is a home, while his
heart is an inn!

There's a beautiful toast
To the feminine host—
There's a swing to "the ladies—God bless 'em,"
But the women should cry
With their glasses on high,
A toast to the men who dress 'em!

I drink to the general joy of the
whole table!

A lass and a glass and a good share of brass,
With a wallet of gold to jingle,
   May we never see double
   If there should be trouble,
And may we be virtuous and single.

———

May the consolation of rectitude sweeten the bitterness of sorrow.

———

To the man of many virtues, if he is not a bore.

———

May we never envy those who are happy, but strive to imitate them.

———

   To the men who strive to reach
   The men to whom they preach.

YESTERDAY'S yesterday
while to-day's here,
To-day is to-day till to-morrow appear,
To-morrow's to-morrow until to-day's past,
And kisses are kisses as long as they last.

 ere's to all faithful and true brothers.

———

As we meet upon the level, may we part upon the square.

———

May the bark of friendship never founder on the rocks of deceit.

———

May the wings of liberty never lose a feather.

———

May we all travel through the world and sow it thick with friendship.

———

May the blush of conscious innocence ever deck the faces of the fair Americans.

MAY
Dame Fortune ever smile
on you;
But never her daughter—
Miss Fortune.

 to champagne, the drink
divine,
That makes us forget our
troubles :
'Tis made of a dollar's worth of wine
And three dollars' worth of bubbles.

May we kiss whom we please,
And please whom we kiss

To those who bring sunshine into the lives
of others, and cannot keep it from themselves

I have met many, liked a few ;
Loved but one—here's to you.

Here's to the prettiest,
Here's to the wittiest,
Here's to the truest of all
who are true.
Here's to the neatest one,
Here's to the sweetest one,
Here's to them all in one—
here's to you.

———

Here's to Woman—
First she makes our heart
Then wakes it,
So breaks it,
Then takes it,
Thus mends it,
That ends it.

Here's to the elf of my childhood,
   Here's to the maid of my youth;
  Here's to the girl who gave me her hand,
   But refused me her lips, forsooth!

GOD made man
    Frail as a bubble;
God made love,
    Love made trouble;
God made the vine,
    Was it a sin
That man made wine
    To drown trouble in?

ERE'S that ye may
never die
nor be kilt till ye break your bones over
a bushel o' glory.

HERE'S to the glass we love to sip;
It dries many a pensive tear:
'Tis not so sweet as a woman's lip,
But a blamed sight more sincere.

———

May Sincerity ever quaff the
toast that Friendship proposes!

———

Let us drink to the thought that where'er a man roves
He is sure to find something blissful and dear,
And that when he is far from the lips that he loves
He can always make love to the lips that are near.

———

The man sat on the moonlit deck,
His head was in a whirl;
His eyes and mouth were full of hair,
His arms were full of girl.

Here's to Woman—gentle, patient, self-denying; without her man would be a savage, and the earth a desert.

———

May the pleasures of youth never bring us pain in old age.

———

"God bless us, every one."

———

Friendly may we part, and quickly meet again.

———

May every man be what he thinks himself to be.

———

May the hinges of hospitality never creak.

———

May we never know want till relief is at hand.

Here's a toast to all who
are here,
No matter where you're
from:
May the best day you have seen
Be worse than your worst to come.

———

Drink ye to her that each loves best;
And if you nurse a flame
That's told but to her mutual breast,
We will not ask her name.

———

May every mirror we look at cast an honest
reflection.

———

May goodness prevail when beauty fails.

YOU may run the whole gamut of color and shade, A pretty girl, however you dress her, Is the prettiest thing that ever was made, And the last one is always the prettiest, Bless her.

Now, boys, just a moment!
    You've all had your say;
While enjoying ourselves
    In so pleasant a way,
We have toasted our sweethearts,
    Our friends, and our wives;
We've toasted each other,
    Wishing all merry lives;
But I now will propose to you
    The toast that is best—
'Tis one in a million,
    And outshines the rest.
Don't frown when I tell you
    This toast beats all others;
But drink one more toast, boys,—
    A toast to—"Our Mothers."

HERE'S to the tears of friendship! May they crystalize as they fall, and be worn as bright jewels on the bosoms of those we love!

Here's to one another and one other.

Here's to the girls we have
loved who married
other fellows.

May our distinguishing mark be merit rather than
money.

May virtue find fortune always an attendant.

May all single men be married,
And all married men be happy.

May all your troubles be little ones.

 to those I love ;
Here's to those who
love me ;
Here's to those who love those I love,
And here's to those who love those who
love me.

———

May we have the unspeakable good Fortune to
win a true heart, and the Merit to keep it.

———

A cheerful glass, a pretty lass,
A friend sincere and true,
Blooming health, good store of wealth,
Attend on me and you.

WOMAN—the Morning Star of
      infancy,
The Day Star of manhood, and the
      Evening Star of old age.
Bless our stars, and may they always
      be kept at a telescopic distance.

Here's wishing us more friends,
　　And less need of them.

———

Here's to a temperance supper,
　　With water in glasses tall,
And coffee and tea to end with—
　　And me not there at all.

———

Here's to those who love us,
　　If we only cared;
Here's to those we'd love,
　　If we only dared.

———

Here's to the American Eagle, the liberty bird
that permits no liberties.

Here's health to the maiden and
health to the dame,
And health to the little gay widow
the same;
May the maid become dame, the dame widow,
and then
May the widow be made to get married
again!

Here's to the land we love, and the "love" we "land."

———

May the chicken never be hatched that will scratch on your grave.

———

May we live in pleasure and die out of debt.

———

May we always command success by deserving it.

———

May the present meeting be oft repeated.

———

May honesty never be ashamed of an unfashionable garment.

———

May we never make matrimony a matter of money.

re's to our wives and sweethearts:
May they never meet.

———

Here's to sweethearts and wives: may the former
soon become the latter, and the latter never cease
to be the former.

———

Here's to the ladies, God bless 'em!
And here's to their eyes that kindle the
only fire that has no insurance.

———

Here's to man, God's first thought,
Here's to woman, God's second thought;
As second thoughts are best, "Here's to
woman."

Woman—Let us not forget that wherever man is most enlightened, she is most respected and beloved.

———

To perfect woman, nobly planned,
To warn, to comfort, and command.

———

To our fathers' sweethearts—our mothers.

———

Here's to the wife who doesn't sit up.

———

To the chaperons who can be deaf, dumb, and blind.

———

May we look forward with pleasure, and backward without regret.

Here's to the girl
who's bound
to win
Her share, at least, of
blisses,
Who knows enough
not to go in
When it is raining
kisses.

Here's to all of us.
    For there's so much
    good in the worst of us,
And so much bad in the
    best of us,
That it hardly behooves any of us
To talk about the rest of us.

Drink to-day and drown all
sorrow,
You shall perhaps not do it to-
morrow,
But while you have it use your
breath,
There is no drinking after death

———

Here's to American valor:
May no war require it, but may it ever be
ready for every foe.

———

To the ministers who don't preach, and the
preachers who minister.

Woman.

The fairest work of the great Author. The edition is large, and no man should be without a copy.

The Frenchman loves his native wine;
  The German loves his beer;
The Englishman loves his 'alf and 'alf,
  Because it brings good cheer;
The Irishman loves his " whisky straight,"
  Because it gives him dizziness;
The American has no choice at all,
  So he drinks the whole blamed business.

Champagne to our real friends.   Real pain to
our sham friends.

Adam's ale: and may so pure an element
always be at hand.

Here's to the club
girl,
Here's to the tub girl,
Here's to the lass who looks you through;
Here's to the mannish girl,
Here's to the clannish girl,
Drink to 'em standing—the petticoat
crew!

Come, my old friend, and take a pot;
But mark now what I say:
Whilst thou drink thy neighbor's health,
Drink not thine own away.

———

To the Wife—The woman who is expected to purchase without means, and sew on buttons before they come off.

———

We may live without poetry, music, and art,
We may live without conscience and live without
    heart;
We may live without friends, we may live without
    books,
But civilized men cannot live without cooks.

A FULL tumbler to every good fellow, a good tumble to every bad one.

Wine enough to sharpen wit; wit enough to give zest to wine; wisdom to "shut down" at the right time.

———

To the early bird that catches the worm.

———

Here's to the man who never quarrels with his bread and butter.

———

To Good Wives:

> Good wives to snails should be akin,
> Always their houses keep within;
> But not to carry (Fashion's hacks!)
> All they are worth upon their backs.

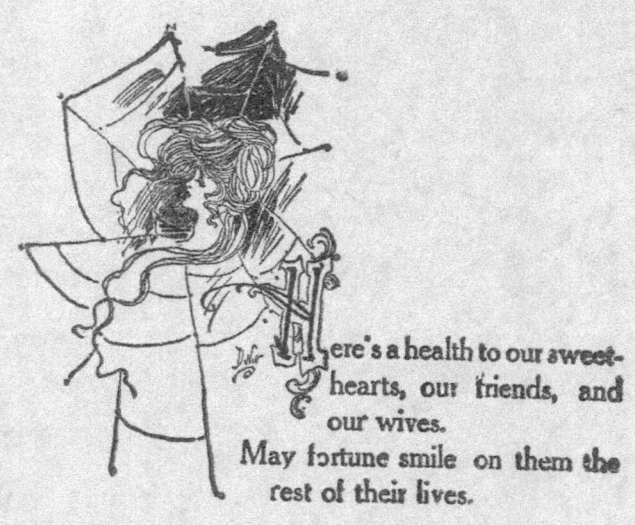

ere's a health to our sweethearts, our friends, and our wives. May fortune smile on them the rest of their lives.

Woman—The *alpha-omega* of man's existence; the mainspring of his every action; the joy and torment of his life; the absolute tyrant whose subjects are slaves, whose slightest caprice is law, and from whose distinction there's no appeal. Yet God grant that her reign may last forever!

———

This world that we're a-livin' in
 Is mighty hard to beat,
For you get a thorn with every rose—
 But ain't the roses sweet!

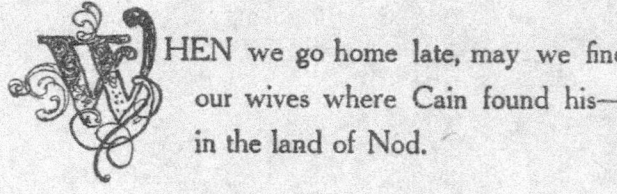HEN we go home late, may we find
our wives where Cain found his—
in the land of Nod.

———

Here's to the friends both near and far,
Here's to woman, man's guiding star;
Here's to friends we've yet to meet,
Here's to all here, all here I greet.
Here's to childhood, youth, old age,
Here's to prophet, bard, and sage;
Here's a health to every one,
Peace on earth and heaven won.

———

To our Sweethearts and Wives.
The bubbles rise less joyously
    To sparkling brim, in ready mirth,
Than to our lips this health; as we
    Drink to the sweetest toast on earth.

May the devil cut the toes off
all our foes,
That we may know them by the
limping.

———

Here's to the world, the merry old world,
To its days both bright and blue;
Here's to our future, be what it may,
And here's to my best—that's you.

———

Here's to you, as good as you are;
Here's to me, as bad as I am;
But as good as you are, and as bad as I am,
I'm as good as you are, as bad as I am.

———

The good die young.
Here's hoping you may live to a ripe old age.

HERE'S to the girl who's
strictly in it,
Who doesn't lose her
head for a minute,
Plays well the game and
knows the limit,
And still gets all the fun
there's in it.

Come in the evening, or come in the morning,
Come when you're looked for, come without
    warning;
A thousand welcomes you'll find here before you!
And the oftener you come the more I'll adore you.

———

A camel can go eight days without a drink,
but who wants to be a camel?

You may drink to her eyes, her
    lips, and her hair,
Her form divine, distingue air;
But here's to a girl with a heart
    and a smile,
Who makes this bubble of
    life worth while!

HERE's a sigh for those that love me,
And a smile for those that hate,
And whatever sky's above me,
Here's a heart for any fate.

———

Come, old fellow, drink down to your peg,
But do not drink any further, I beg.

———

May genius and merit never want a friend.

———

Then fill the cup, fill high! fill high!
Let joy our goblets crown;
We'll bung Misfortune's scowling eye,
And knock Foreboding down.

Here's to the years that are
stretching ahead,
To the days that are blithe-
some and gay.
May the joys of the old be the joys
of the new,
And the sorrows fade gently
away.

There's death in the cup—
sae beware!
Nay, more—there is
danger in touching;
But wha can avoid the
fell snare?
The man and his wine sae bewitching.

To the most perfect gentleman I ever saw;
he turned his back on me—while I poured
myself a drink from his own decanter.

Here's to a good
meal when
you're hungry,
And good wine when you're dry,
The pretty girl who loves you,
And heaven when you die.

———

To Hope—A pleasant acquaintance, but an unsafe
friend,
A good traveling companion, but not
the man for one's banker.

———

Now the fair goddess, Fortune,
Fall deep in love with thee.

HERE'S to woman, whose heart and soul
Are the light and life of each spell we pursue;
Whether sunn'd at the tropics or chilled at the pole,
If women be there, there is happiness too.

And let the Loving-Cup go round,
The cup with blessed memories crowned,
That flows whene'er we meet, my boys.
No draught will hold a drop of sin,
If love is only well stirred in
To keep it sound and sweet, my boys,
To keep it sound and sweet.

A health, gentlemen,
Let it go round.

Come, let's drink while we have breath,
For there's no drinking after death.

As we travel through life may we live well
on the road.

HERE's to woman, the
source of our bliss;
There's a forestaste of
heaven in her kiss;
But from the queen upon her
throne to the maiden in the
dairy,
They are all alike, in one respect—contrary!

Wine, women, mirth,
and laughter,
Sermons and soda water
the day after.

Some hae meat and canna' eat,
And some wad eat who want it;
But we hae meat and we can eat,
So let the Lord be thankit.

Here's to the lasses we've loved, my lad,
Here's to the lips we've pressed:
For of kisses and lasses,
Like liquor in glasses,
The last is always the best.

I'll give a toast
        To a strange host,
    Who are to a man true topers,
        I think.
    Here's to the tramps,
        Those vagrant scamps,
Who drink what they can, and "can" what they drink.

The American Eagle and the Thanksgiving Turkey.
    May one give us peace in all our States,
    And the other a piece for all our plates.

May those who enter the rosy paths of matrimony
        never meet with thorns.

    Here's to the bride that is to be,
        Happy and smiling and fair,
    And here's to those who would like to be,
        And are wondering when and where.

ere's to our wives—
They keep our lives in little bees
and honey.
They darn our socks, and save
life's shocks,
And they also spend our money.

———

Pat may be foolish
And sometimes very wrong;
Pat has a temper
Which don't last very long;
Pat is full of jollity,
That everybody knows,
And you'll never find a coward
Where the Shamrock grows.

———

May every day bring more happiness than yesterday.

THE way ain't sunny,
But don't you fret!
Cheer up, honey—
You'll get there yet!

HERE'S to me!—

mamma's pet and pop's boast,
To my solos at night, which they roast!
To my pug little nose
And my ten curly toes!
How's that for a little Milk Toast?

Here's to the happiest days of
my life,
Spent in the lap of
another man's wife:
My mother.

ove to one, friendship to a few, and good will to all.

———

May we always mean well, and act accordingly.

———

'Tis easy enough to be pleasant
When life glides by like a song;
But the man worth while
Is the man who can smile
When everything goes dead wrong.

———

May our actions ever evince this belief, that honesty is the best policy.

———

May the difference of creeds be ever left at the house of prayer.

———

Here's short shoes and long corns to our enemies.

HERE'S to solitaire with
a partner,
The only game in which
one pair beats three
of a kind.

HERE'S to the glad-
ness of her gladness when
she's glad,
Here's to the sadness of her sadness when she's sad;
But the gladness of her gladness,
And the sadness of her sadness,
Are not in it with the madness of her madness
when she's mad.

———

Once more fill a bumper—never talk of the hour;
Our hearts thus united, old Time has no power.
May our lives, tho' alas!—like the wine of to-night,
They must soon have an end—to the last, flow as
bright.

———

No chord of music has yet been found
To even equal that sweet sound
Which, to my mind, all else surpasses,
The clink of ice in crystal glasses.

 your soul be in glory three weeks before the devil knows you're dead.

————

Here's to the girls we've asked, old pal.
　Here's to the girls who said nay.
'Tis better for us they treated us thus,
　For they're driving the Mormons away.

————

"I wish," he said, "you could make pies
　Like mother used to bake."
"And I," said she, "wish that you made
　The dough pa used to make!"

————

Here's to the two of you, and may you be
so close, that either one of you will be only
half of you; so here's to you two as one pie

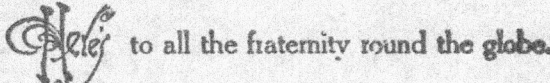 to all the fraternity round the globe.

———

May every brother have a heart to feel and a hand to give.

———

May the brethren of our glorious craft be ever distinguished in the world by their regular lives more than by their gloves and aprons.

———

Every brother who keeps the key of knowledge from intruders, but cheerfully gives it to a worthy brother.

———

May prosperity never make us arrogant, nor adversity, mean.

———

May we live happy and die in peace with all mankind.

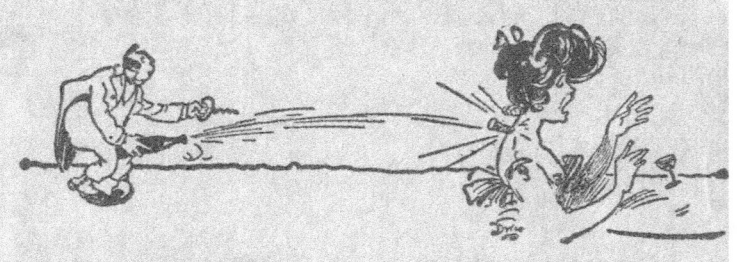

'Ere's to the 'ealth o' your Royal 'Ighness; hand may the skin o' ha gooseberry be big enough for han humbrella to cover up hall your henemies.

Here's to the maiden of bashful fifteen;
    Here's to the widow of fifty;
Here's to the flaunting, extravagant queen,
    And here's to the housewife that's thrifty.
        Let the toast pass,
        Drink to the lass,
I'll warrant she'll prove an excuse for the glass.

HERE'S to Uncle Sam: the most respected, genial, farcical, picturesque, courteous, gallant, hospitable, generous, liberty-loving, calm, judicial, honorable, misunderstood old myth that ever was invented.

We hope you have enjoyed this book, compiled by Wm. Rhoads in the early 1900s, published in 1904 by the Penn Publishing Company in Philadelphia, and preserved here.

The illustrations were rendered by Clare Victor Dwiggins. Dwiggins began as an architect, but found success as a cartoonist in the early 1900s.

The original book of TOASTS is shaped like a beer stein and bears a soft leather cover.

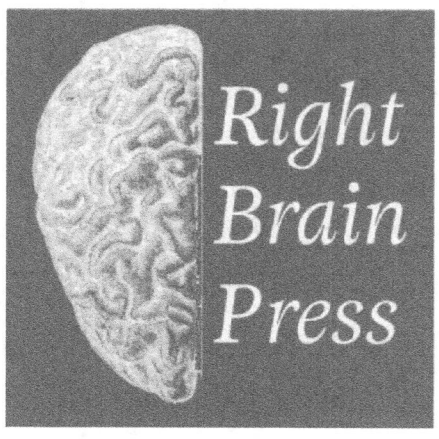

Right Brain Press